CLASSY SASSY AND A BIT BAD ASSY

We are brave, we are strong, and we are not to be messed with. Rekindle your fierce spirit with this empowering collection of inspirational quotes and life-affirming statements.

IF I WAS MEANT TO BE CONTROLLED, I'D HAVE COME WITH A REMOTE.

CLASSY SASSY AND A BIT BAD ASSY ♀

An Hachette UK Company
www.hachette.co.uk

First published in Great Britain in 2021 by Pyramid,
an imprint of Octopus Publishing Group Ltd
Carmelite House, 50 Victoria Embankment,
London EC4Y 0DZ
www.octopusbooks.co.uk

Distributed in the US by
Hachette Book Group
1290 Avenue of the Americas
4th and 5th Floors
New York, NY 10104

Distributed in Canada by
Canadian Manda Group
664 Annette St.
Toronto, Ontario, Canada M6S 2C8

ISBN 978-07537-3456-8

A CIP catalogue record for this book is available from
the British Library

Printed and bound in China

10 9 8 7 6 5 4 3 2 1

you have what
it takes.
it's your turn.
don't waste
any more time.
get busy and
kick ass.

some girls
are just born
with glitter
in their veins

I DO A THING CALLED "WHAT I WANT"

throw sass
like it's confetti

BE BOLD
BE BRAVE
BE FEARLESS
BE YOURSELF

TELL ME NOT TO DO SOMETHING AND I'LL DO IT TWICE AND TAKE PICTURES

*what is a queen without
her king?*

*well, historically
speaking, more powerful.*

NO NEED TO HURRY, NO NEED TO SPARKLE, NO NEED TO BE ANYBODY BUT ONESELF.

VIRGINIA WOOLF

If I say:
"first of all",
run away fast
because I
have prepared
research and
data and
charts and I
am going to
destroy you

if you can't handle
me at my worst, don't
forget that I can
and that makes me
stronger than you.

YOU CAN BE
ON MY SIDE
BY MY SIDE
OR IN MY WAY

CHOOSE WISELY

behind every great man stands no woman. there is no greater man than the man that can acknowledge the woman standing right next to him.

STRONG WOMEN DON'T HAVE ATTITUDES.

THEY HAVE STANDARDS.

throw me to
the wolves
and I'll come
back leading
the pack

IT'S NOT AN ATTITUDE, IT'S THE WAY I AM.

YOU CAN'T
DO EPIC SHIT
WITH BASIC PEOPLE

BEFORE YOU JUDGE ME, YOU'D BETTER MAKE SURE YOU'RE PERFECT.

WAKE UP BEAUTY, IT'S TIME TO BEAST.

well-behaved women seldom make history

eleanor roosevelt

If you're
going to test
my waters,
you'd better
know how to swim.

WHEN PEOPLE ASK ME WHAT I DO, I TELL THEM I DO WHATEVER IT TAKES.

TREAT ME LIKE A JOKE AND I'LL LEAVE YOU LIKE IT'S FUNNY

ONCE IN A WHILE BLOW YOUR OWN DAMN MIND

she is both hell fire
and holy water.
which you taste will
depend on how you
treat her.

The truth will set you free. But first, it will piss you off.

Gloria Steinem

YOU WANTED FIRE? SORRY, MY SPECIALTY IS ICE

VERONICA LODGE

THEY WATCH
THEN THEY HATE
THEN THEY COPY

BE SAVAGE
NOT AVERAGE

I would have girls
regard themselves
not as adjectives,
but as nouns.

Elizabeth Cady Stanton

You're not gonna tell me who I am.

I'm gonna tell you who I am.

TAKE ME
AS I AM
OR WATCH
ME AS I GO

A SASS A DAY KEEPS THE BASICS AWAY

don't
get
bitter,
just
get
better.

alyssa edwards

please don't ever think that I need you in my life because at one point we didn't know each other and I was doing fine.

BE YOU, DO YOU, FOR YOU.

conquer from within

life is too short for fake butter, cheese or people.

NO PRESSURE, NO DIAMONDS.

my lips are
the gun,
my smile is
the trigger,
my kisses
are the
bullets, label
me a killer

I'm not always sarcastic, sometimes I'm sleeping.

that stone you are about to throw better hit me because I've got a brick for you

don't play with me
because I know I
can play better than
you and that makes
me very dangerous

THE BEST REVENGE IS
MASSIVE SUCCESS

I will fight for you
but I will not
compete for you.

There's a difference.

Sometimes you gotta be the Beauty AND the Beast

*there is no competition,
because nobody can be me.*

SEEK RESPECT, NOT ATTENTION.

you used to be my cup of tea but I drink champagne now.

CATCH FLIGHTS NOT FEELINGS

SWEET AS SUGAR
HARD AS ICE
HURT ME ONCE
I'LL KILL YOU TWICE

a girl should be
two things:
who and what
she wants.

coco chanel

KILL THEM WITH SUCCESS, BURY THEM WITH A SMILE.

there is no
gate, no lock,
no bolt that
you can set
upon the
freedom of
my mind.

virginia woolf

no, this isn't a dream, this is my reality.

when in doubt, freak 'em out.

Sharon Needles

STAY REAL, STAY LOYAL, OR STAY THE HELL AWAY FROM ME.

girls compete,
women empower.

They say good things come to those who wait, which is why I'm always late.

BITCHES GET STUFF DONE

TINA FEY

a wise girl knows her limits, a smart girl knows she has none.

marilyn monroe

GOOD VIBES OR GOODBYE

work for
a cause,
not for
applause.
live life to
express.
not to
impress.

CANCEL MY SUBSCRIPTION BECAUSE I AM DONE WITH YOUR ISSUES.

If I cut you off, it's likely you handed me the scissors.

MY ATTITUDE
IS SAVAGE
BUT MY
HEART IS
GOLD

**chin up princess,
or the crown slips.**

KINDA CLASSY
KINDA HOOD

a wise woman
once said
"f*ck this sh*t"
and lived
happily
ever after

darling I'm a nightmare dressed like a daydream

taylor swift

EAT

PRAY

SLAY

in order
for you to
insult me I
must first
value your
opinion.

But I don't.

die with memories,
not dreams.

**no one expects an angel
to set the world on fire**

behind every
successful
woman is a tribe
of women who
have her back

KNOW YOUR WORTH, THEN ADD TAX.

be like a butterfly: pretty to see, hard to catch.

HUSTLE UNTIL YOUR HATERS ASK IF YOU'RE HIRING

your mind is a weapon.
keep it open.

you can
never go
wrong with a
little pink...
a lot works
too.

DIFFICULT WOMEN CONQUER DIFFICULT THINGS

DON'T MAKE CHOICES, MAKE MOVES.

there is no force more
powerful than a woman
determined to rise

My coach said I ran like a girl, and I said that if he ran a little faster, he could too.

Mia Hamm

when the sun goes down, I glow up.

I NEVER LOSE.
EITHER I WIN,
OR I LOSE.

Don't mistake my kindness for weakness

OBEY ALL THE RULES, MISS ALL THE FUN.

IF YOU LISTEN CAREFULLY, YOU CAN HEAR ME NOT CARING

it's about time.
where's my
throne?

be your own
reason to smile